# Potential To Be
# SUPERPOWER

MANGESH DAMBHARE

# DEDICATION

Hare Kṛṣṇa Hare Kṛṣṇa

Kṛṣṇa Kṛṣṇa Hare Hare
Hare Rāma Hare Rāma
Rāma Rāma Hare Hare

# CONTENTS

# PREFACE

After reading this book you will start understanding the potential of India to become a superpower in the near future. India has the leading mindset and intellect since the millenniums back in history. Archeological surveys have already discovered the historic existence of advanced civilizations in the Indus valley region.

History will repeat again with the establishment of advanced and intellectual Indian civilization by the revival of the glorious period of India.

This book is an overlook on the capabilities of India to become a superpower nation that will play a major role in the development of human societies and world peace.

# 1 ANCIENT INDIA

# Advanced Vedic Civilization

India was covered with the historical kingdoms having constituents like individual's intellect, developed societies, royal lifestyles, and innovations.

With the creations of Vedas and other scriptures sages in the early period formed the base of disciplined, very truthful, powerful, and multitalented generations. People were having love, affection, gratitude, compassion, and loyalty with the family, society, and with the administration also.

It was the era of many evolutions and creations like scriptures and temples of Vedic traditions setting up norms for the ethical and ideological behavior of whole mankind.

Regions saw many high-profile kings, artists, writers, inventors, and skilled professionals. There were many supernatural incarnations (Avatars) of Gods and Goddesses in this region of the planet, along with many saints and great disciples. The footprints of their creative works and teachings still giving directions to mankind with positive energy.

# Great Scriptures

Teachings of Hinduism are very prolific and can be learned from different Hindu Scriptures. In the early period of civilization, sages have played an important role in the creations of the great scriptures.

Those great scriptures are Vedas (Rigveda, Samaveda, Yajurveda, Atharvaveda), Upanishads, Maha Purana, Major Puranas, Minor Puranas, Samhitas, Ramayana, Mahabharata, Srimad Bhagavad Gita, Srimad Bhagavatam, etc.

From time to time many views on Srimad Bhagwat Gita were documented by the experts. Literature of Kalidasa in Sanskrit language and Writings of Chanakya on good governance and public administration are notable historical creations.

# Foresight

Indian thinkers and authors in the early historical period were having deep study and a foresight for the upcoming generations of the ages. They had set rules for good practices and methodologies for living the life with better standards.

But unfortunately, world lacks in paying enough attention towards the creations and writings of these ancient intellectual sages on this planet.

Now the time has come and there is a great demand to listen to the early historical bases of values, knowledge, and superior ideologies in the history of mankind.

# 2 ETERNAL EVOLUTIONS

# Spirituality

Spirituality is the essence of life; it is the source of all of the divine power. Learning methods and teachings of spirituality are the ways to come out of all pain and suffering in materialistic expectations.

Concepts in spirituality were put forth before the world in the early historic period of India. Religions in India have been giving lessons of spirituality to the world since ancient times.

# Yoga

Yoga is one of the most precious practices that evolved in Hindu traditions. You will find a dynamic change in your life if you practice these in your life.

Sage Patanjali has given us teachings of Yoga through his creation 'Yoga Sutras of Patanjali'. It is constituted of eight limbs; those are Yamas, Niyama, Āsana, Prāṇāyāma, Pratyāhāra, Dhāraṇā, Dhyāna, Samādhi.

The concepts of Yoga described in the Shrimad Bhagwat Gita are related to action, devotion, and knowledge. It shows the path to lead a life with success using one of these paths.

# Ayurveda

India has given the world the gift of care through the evolution of Ayurveda. It is related to health practices using yoga, herbal compounds, and natural extracts of minerals.

Charaka Samhita and Sushruta Samhita are the main source of all studies related to Ayurveda. It deals with various Chikitsas, Tantras, and Methods of Panchkarma.

# Sanskrit

India has 122 major languages and more than 1500 spoken languages. Some major Indic languages are Hindi, Bengali, Marathi, Telgu, Tamil, Gujrati, Punjabi, and Sanskrit.

Sanskrit is one of the oldest languages in the world and most ancient epics and scriptures are found written in the Sanskrit Language. Sanskrit is being studied not in India but also in prominent universities in the world.

The Grammar of Panini, especially 'Astadhyayi' written by him are the important texts for learning Sanskrit Grammar.

18

# Literature

The foundations for structures of the study related to the literature have been made during early historic periods of India.

Literary works by Kalidasa and Adi Sankara along with many Sanskrit authors can be seen through the books about Sanskrit Literature consisting of dramas and poems

# Education System

Creation of such ethical, brave, and glorious ancient societies and kingdoms of India was only the result of a great educational system existed at that time.

'Gurukula Parampara' was the established advanced education system in Ancient India which has no challenge and can prove the best today also if implemented with some modern modifications.

# Religion

Hinduism referred to 'Sanātana Dharma' is the most ancient and oldest religion in the world and the way of a beautiful life evolved in India. Every traditions and festivals in Hindu culture are having scientific bases; most of them are being proved right with respect to circumstances and time. Hinduism has evolutionary and persistent thoughts of culture.

The first millennium was the period of religious evolutions and establishments. There were peaceful coexistences of Hinduism, Buddhism, Islam, and Christianity in the world.

# Culture

Indus Valley Civilization dated approximately 4,000 years ago is considered as the most advanced ancient civilization in the history of the world according to the findings by archeological surveys.

In the history of India Vedic culture has great importance. Creations of Vedic texts like Vedas, Upanishads, and The Grammar of Panini were significant in the history of mankind.

Evolutions of Indian Classical Music and Dance are precious gifts to the world.

26

# Diversity

Varied cultures and traditions are found within India since long time back in the history. From north to south and east to west, India has different regions with specific languages, dialects, cultures, and traditions those add colors in the wings of this great nation.

Diverse flora and fauna, geographical landmarks, forests and rivers, seas and coastal beauty, and the glorious mountains of the Himalayas are the part of the physical existence of the great soul of the nation.

28

# 3 GLORIOUS HISTORY

# Kingdoms

In the history of India you can see lots of great empires and kingdoms with mighty and brave Kings ruled and win over the heart of people and created glorious history.

During the ancient times in India, the Ikshvaku dynasty also called as Solar dynasty gave great rulers like Bharata, Harishchandra, Raghu, and Rama. The legendary lunar dynasty consisted of Puru, Yadu, Anu, and Krishna.

Some of the notable post-Vedic historical kingdoms in the region were Nanda, Maurya, Kushan, Satvahana, Gupta, Chalukya, Chola, etc.

32

# Mahajanpadas

Mahajanpadas were the great kingdoms in the regions of India during the early historical period. Those were Kashi, Kosala, Kuru, Panchala, Magadha, Gandhara, Kamboja, Malla, Assaka, Matsya, Anga, Chedi, Surasena, Avanti, Vatsa, and Vriji

# Gold and Prosperity

The historical period of India before the second millennium was very glorious and advanced with the prosperity of resources, living lifestyles of the peoples pertaining values and traditions. The societies were ethically idealistic, developed, wealthy and very rich.

# Great Architects

There had been constructions of many astonishing and creatively build temples in India before the second millennium. Today also you can move all over India to see such beautiful and great creations of early historical architects.

# Early Universities

University of ancient Taxila, Nalanda University, and The School of Pushpagiri were among the advanced learning centers well established in India before the second millennium. They were among the initial universities in the world.

# 4 TO BE A SUPERPOWER

# Economy

## Rise of India

India is one of the top economies which influence businesses all over the world. India will surpass China until 2035 if the growth of India's Economy will soar high. Financial reforms by the government of India 2014 onwards and entrepreneurs' rising aspirations in India are creating potential and grounds for sustainable growth in the upcoming future. Business-friendly policies and the new educational policy will act as reviving agents in boosting the economy.

## Economic Self-Sufficient

Atmanirbhar Bharat is an initiative of the Government of India to promote Micro, Small & Medium Enterprises (MSMEs) by providing economic assistance and encouragements. Its objective is to encourage creating an influence of the indigenous products and businesses at the international level and making them more competent.

# Military Capability

### Capabilities

Armed with zealous patriotism and the toughest combating skills with large multitalented active troops, Indian defence forces are ready to conquer any challenges to world peace. India is emerging as a global power player in the defence sector with world-class armed preparations and strategic planning. India has the capability to lead the world in outlining strategic defence plans and policies. It has the strong capability to deter the aggressions against the humanities.

Latest military reforms, enough military spending, major arms importer and exporter, and building strategic defence partnerships with the nations on the ground of common interest are key strengths of India's Military Capabilities. India is a powerful command in the strategically important Indian Ocean Region.

India has indomitable armed forces with Special Frontier Force, Marine & Garud Commandos, and Ghatak Force. As a defence power equipped with advanced fighter aircrafts like Rafale, Sukhoi 30 Mirage 2000, and HAL Tejas, Nuclear-Capable Indian Ballistic Missile Defence Programme, and

World-Class Submarines, India can deter any military might on this planet.

## Alliance

India has maintained good and strategic relations with all major counties and power blocks in the world. India is an active participant of The Quadrilateral Security Dialogue Forum between the United States, Japan, Australia, and India. India has also maintained good relations with Russia, Israel, France, Vietnam and some Gulf countries. India held many joint military exercises with the United States, Japan, Russia, France, Kazakhstan, Mongolia and also was two times participant of Exercise Red Flag by the United States Air Force.

# Young Talent

There are more than 700 universities and more than 40,000 colleges in India. They have a good educational infrastructure with advanced facilities like laboratories and libraries.

These educational facilities, technological assistance, and traditional intellectual inheritance of knowledge with experiences are creating a pool of new age young generations full of talents and creativity.

# Leading IT Hub

India generates most of the IT brains, talents, executives, and high-profile CEOs throughout the globe. India has a growing number of several IT companies, software industries, and IT parks. India is also a huge market for online web-based industries and brands.

Software Development, App Development, Cloud Computing, Financial Technology, Information Architecture, Internet of Things (IoT), Artificial Intelligence (AI), and Research & Development in Advance Computing in such every field India is leading the world.

# 5 BECOMING VISHWA GURU

52

# Yoga and Health

India is a land of 'Yogis' from ancient times and enriched with all the resources of spirituality and ways of living life in a beautiful and powerful manner.

Yoga is very helpful for the recreations of the mind and thoughts. Just practice for few days and you could see some positive changes in your health conditions.

Every year 21st June is being celebrated as International Yoga Day.

54

# Ayurveda

Ayurveda is an alternative medical health science being practiced in India since the Vedic period. It is very eco-friendly and has no side. Usage and practices of Ayurveda are growing day by day throughout the world.

# Spirituality

India has constantly delivered a flow of spiritual knowledge to the world in all forms. From the early historical presentations and formations of spiritual concepts to the modern day's revival, India has always shown the right direction to the world.

# New Educational Policy

India has an enormous well established educational structure of study materials and learning institutions. New Educational Policy proposed by Indian Government will transform India into an educational epicenter of the world.

Colleges and universities in India are already demonstrating a great role on the world stage. Indian Institute of Technology (IITs), Indian Institute of Management (IIMs), All India Institute Of Medical Science (AIIMS), Film and Television Institute of India (FTII), National Defence Academy (NDA), Armed Forces Medical College (AFMC), College of Military Engineering (COME) are the prestigious Institutions in India creating a pool of talents who leads various sectors around the globe with their superior brain capacity.

# Global Leadership

Indians are leading the way of living standards full of values and ethics. They are creating success stories of expertise and presentations with international standards and achieving global recognition to their works and creativity.

India is proactively participating and contributing in all important global initiatives by United Nations Organizations, World Health Organizations, and World Trade Organizations. India has an important role and in the consideration of policies and reforms by mostly all international organizations of countries.

# Friendly Policies

Business-friendly policies introduced by the government of India will act as reviving agents in boosting the economy. Foreign investors are showing great confidence in the business environment in India and they are seeing financial growth and prospect to invest in India.

# Efforts for World Peace

India is a major contributor to the United Nations peacekeeping forces and participates in mostly all peace missions. India plays an important role in world politics.

India has a peace-loving mindset, never offended other countries, and shown great respect for the sovereignty of other nations.

# 6 WORLD CLASS INFRASTUCTURE

# Infrastructure Projects

The National Infrastructure Pipeline is a set of proposed infrastructure projects for energy, rail projects, highway projects, and urban development projects.

# Roads and Bridges

Bharatmala project consists of the Golden Quadrilateral, National Highway Development Project, North-South and East-West Corridors, Char Dham Highway, Yamuna Expressway, and The Diamond Quadrilateral.

There are ongoing constructions of the expressway at major highways and Setu Bharatam project which is considered of building flyovers on all national highways at all railway crossings across India.

Mumbai Trans Harbour Link, Eastern Freeway, and Sewri – Worli Connector are the ambitious projects in Mumbai, India.

# Railways

Works of creating dedicated freight corridors and modern rail stations are underway.

The Diamond Quadrilateral is a project of developing a high-speed network among the four metro cities across India.

Western Dedicated Freight Corridor and Eastern Dedicated Freight Corridor are under construction and will be completed before 2023.

# Shipyards

Sagarmala project is proposed to create waterways and ports across all major places along the coastline of India. It consists of the development of fourteen major coastal economic zones to boost economic activities along the ports. There is also a projection of development related to Inland Waterways in India.

# Aviation

India has near about 34 International Airports and more than 450 airports in the country. Navi Mumbai International Airport and Noida International Greenfield Airport or Jewar Airport are the upcoming planned world-class airport projects in India.

# Hi-tech Cities

Advanced Plan Cities in India are Gujarat International Finance Tec-City (GIFT), Dholera Smart City Projects, and Smart City Kochi etc.

Smart Cities Mission by the Government of India and constructions of several Smart City projects along dedicated freight corridors are the most ambitious plans for New India.

# Mega Structures

Central Vista Redevelopment Project, Chenab Rail Bridge (World's Highest Rail Bridge), The Atal Tunnel (The longest highway tunnel in the world), Pamban Bridge (Connecting Pamban Island and Rameswaram) are the notable mega structures in development phase.

National War Memorial is a great monument spread across 40 acres area of land and dedicated for honoring the sacrifices made by the soldiers in Indian Armed Forces.

# World-Class IT Infrastructures

India has developed Special Economic Zones and infrastructures providing all the required facilities for software firms, tech hubs, innovation centers, and incubators to start-ups. India plays an important role in the global IT sector with a major share of contribution to the world class innovations.

84

# Foodies, Hotels, Malls

A variety of delicious Indian foods and recipes is really awesome and nutritious. You can see lots of food recipes and varieties across all states and regions of India.

Tourism and hotel industries within India are really of international standards. There is all kind of accommodations and lodgings facilities with all types of economical packages.

Lots of Malls and Supermarkets are being operated and constructed within India with new trends.

# Sports Facilities

India has all kind of sport facilities and infrastructure. Indian government is promoting sport culture in India by taking different kind of initiatives.

India has several large and world-class international stadiums. The Narendra Modi Stadium is the largest cricket stadium in the world. Sardar Vallabhbhai Patel Sport Complex in Ahmedabad, Shree Shiv Chhatrapati Sports Complex in Balewadi of Pune, The Yamuna Sports Complex in Delhi, and The Buddh International Circuit in Delhi are the prominent sport facilities in India.

# Agriculture

There is tremendous growth seen in India's agriculture and food sector within the last few years. The use of advanced technologies and advanced farming are creating inspirations and confidence within the farmers in India. India is self-sufficient in homegrown whole grains, pulses, vegetables, and fruits with adequate production and supply. India is one of the major food exporters to the world.

# Manufacturing Industries

India has grown enough in the manufacturing sector. And India is paving the way to be a leading manufacturing hub by promoting the Micro, Small & Medium Enterprises (MSME) sector, taking necessary measures, and boosting the economy. There is also a major growth in foreign direct investments in India within the last few years.

# Tourism

The Statue of Unity, Lotus Temple in Delhi, The Taj Mahal in Agra, Udaipur's City Palace, Mysore Palace, Elephanta Caves are the point of attraction for the tourists all over the world.

# Religious Places

Ancient and holy religious places in India are having amazing and astonishing architectures.

Ganesh Temples, Char Dham, Bara Jyotirlingas, Shakti Peethas, Mathura, Vrindavan, Vitthal Mandir Pandharpur, Tirupathi Balaji, Shri Datta Kshetra Gangapur, Shani Shingnapur, Baba Amarnath, ISKCON Temples, and Swaminarayan Temples are some prominent temples in India.

Kashi Temple and Ghat, Meenakshi Temple in Madurai, Konark Sun Temple, Brihadeeswarar Temple at Thanjavur, Ranakpur Jain Temple, Golden Temple in Amritsar, Kailasa Temple at Ellora are notable pilgrimages in India.

Shri Ram Temple in Ayodhya, Viraat Ramayan Mandir in Sarangpur, and Shri Vrindavan Chandrodaya Mandir in Vrindavan are the superstructures under construction in india.

# 7 INTELLECTUAL INDIANS

# Political leadership

The great political will of our leader of the nation taking the nation to achieve a new high. In the leadership of Honorable Prime Minister Narendra Modi, India is constantly making good progress towards becoming a Global Superpower. He is very much focused on the planned framework of achievements.

# Business Leaders

Within the last couple of decades, there is an increasing number of Indian business tycoons and leaders. They have created a set up of big industries and businesses across almost all sectors. They are becoming the driving force for the economical growth of the country.

There are growing number of innovators, entrepreneurs, and their indigenous startups in the country those are taking shapes to form the prospects and creating the bright future of the nation.

# Workforce

India has a great number of talents and workforce in the form of doctors, health workers, skilled workers, engineers, architects, professionals, scientists, and researchers. India generates most of the talents and high-profile executives.

# 8 EMERGING SUPERPOWER

# Stepping Milestones

## Powerful Reforms

Major powerful reforms that have been introduced and will be proposed by the Modi government should be studied carefully and understood taking note of its importance. Those can be a guideline for policymakers all over the world.

## Major Reforms

Business-friendly economic reforms, FDI generating reforms, the New Educational Policy, reforms in defense sector, administrative reforms, and all other transforming reforms by the Modi led government will boost the status of the countries progress and development parameters.

## Meeting with the Expectations of the People

All these reforms are placed as fulfilling expectations of the people from their leader and the government. Their hope and desire to be part of a good developed cultural society is sustained by the government under the leadership of Narendra Modi.

# Ready Infra and Facilities

India is getting ready with its advanced new-age infrastructures and public facilities.

Most of the infrastructure projects across the nation in on the way to completion and will be ready before 2023-24. On the other hand, the quality of life and the living standards of the people even in the rural sector are also improving very fast.

Developments are taking shape and very soon India will step ahead by forming a new look with a New India.

# Super Intellectual Society

The lifestyle of the Indians is showing a lot of improvements within the last two decades. Intellectual factor is becoming very common in the understanding of the Indians.

Use of modern technologies and spiritual inclination in the living standard are the qualities which are making some Indians extraordinary.

Ancestral heritage of values and ethics, intellect in work and creativity, and having the modern approach is enough for the creation of super intellectual society with ethics.

# Superpower

India has potential to be a superpower in the near future as a major economy and a powerful defence power in the world.

India's infrastructure projects and economic self-sufficiency will help to achieve the goals.

India started its new sustainable path of development in all aspects. India is progressing on this path on all fronts.

It is very clear that definitely India will influence the world in the coming future in terms of economy, as a global power player, epicenter of spirituality, and cultural heritage.

And India will be one of the superpowers as 'Vishwaguru'.

# ABOUT THE AUTHOR

Mangesh Dambhare is a writer from Yavatmal, Maharashtra, India. He is a graduate of the University of Pune. He is having more than twelve years of expertise in User Interface and User Experience Design. He is a successful Published Author having a Positive, Constructive, and Optimistic Outlook with exposure to the various Media Platforms. The mission of his life is to Empower Humans through his Books and Initiatives.

www.ingramcontent.com/pod-product-compliance
Lightning Source LLC
Chambersburg PA
CBHW070942250726
48663CB00001B/38